Do Your Best EVERY DAY to Do Your Best EVERY DAY

ENCOURAGING WORDS from JOHN CENA

Do Your Best EVERY DAY to Do Your Best EVERY DAY

Illustrations by
SUSANNA HARRISON

Random House 🏠 New York

For Harry, Rose, and Milla,
my shining stars x —S.H.

Copyright © 2021 by John F.A. Cena Entertainment, Inc.

All rights reserved. Published in the United States by
Random House Children's Books, a division of
Penguin Random House LLC, New York.

Random House and the colophon are registered trademarks
of Penguin Random House LLC.

Visit us on the Web! rhcbooks.com

Educators and librarians, for a variety of teaching tools,
visit us at RHTeachersLibrarians.com

Library of Congress Cataloging-in-Publication Data
is available upon request.
ISBN 978-0-593-37722-2 (trade) — ISBN 978-0-593-37723-9 (GLB) —
ISBN 978-0-593-40839-1 (ebook)

The illustrations for this book were created digitally.
The text of this book is set in 12-point Bookman Old Style CE.
Interior design by Katrina Damkoehler

MANUFACTURED IN CHINA
10 9 8 7 6 5 4 3 2 1
First Edition

I am creating this space for you,
the reader, to dedicate this book to
someone or something of meaning
to you. We all have role models,
inspirations, and goals that guide us.

I, _____,

dedicate this book to

_____.

LISTEN UP.

Just a bit of advice from me to you.

Celebrate this.
Celebrate however you can.

Enjoy the moment.
Enjoy achieving the goal.
Enjoy the victory.

You've put in a lot of time and worked
very hard to get where you are.

Do not forget all the things
that brought you here—hard work,
perseverance. Remember the bad times,
remember the good times, the great
friends and the moments you've
shared along the way.

This is the very foundation
for the future of your life.
And your life is the foundation
for the future of humankind.

Don't rush to find out
what you want to be when you grow up.
But when you do find out,
give that goal everything you have,
every day.

Sometimes getting lost
is one of the best ways
to find your destination.

A slow start is better than no start.

The only obstacle
that can slow you down
is not believing in yourself.

Live in each moment,
and use what you've learned
to get you where you want to go.

Never discount the power
of being there for those close to you.
Sometimes the best thing we
can do is *just listen.*

Ask questions.
Challenge norms.
Seek answers to everything in life—
especially to the reflection
staring back at you.
This is very difficult,
but in the end
it is always worth it.

If you never fail,
you will never really know
what you are capable of.

Character is how you behave
when no one is watching.
You are the sum of your actions,
not your words.

Be yourself,
because who you really are
is *a perfect example of you.*

In trying to be liked by everyone,
don't become no one.

If someone takes a chance on you,
prove them right.
Give your all and seize the opportunity.
Be diligent.
Be grateful.

Happiness is achieved by
living your life your way.
Others may not agree with
your actions or choices.
Remember: it's your life, not theirs.
Go forth, live, be happy.

Never be afraid to dream big.
The bigger the dream,
the bigger the effort.

Chasing dreams
requires an incredible amount of work.
Never give up.

We all struggle.
You don't need to struggle alone.
Asking for help is not weakness.

Weakness is a strength.
With so many people worried
about being perfect,
vulnerability and showing weakness
is the absolute key to growth.
Opening up is one of the best ways
to learn about life.

Strength comes from being
brave enough to face fear,
recognize it,
and overcome it
to let YOU shine through!

Stay true to what you believe in.
Be patient.
Know that you will fail.
Be accountable.
Embrace the uncomfortable.
Get back up.

Never lose your ability to imagine.

When you are scared,
afraid,
unsure,
lost,
or even down,
lean on those you love.
The power of love from family and friends
can do amazing things.

43

Each day try to become
a little less perfect
and *a little more brave.*

Do your best every day
to do your best every day.

Whenever possible,
handle challenges
with logic,
kindness,
patience,
and empathy.

Two phrases that have always inspired *me*:
Commitment to excellence.
Adapt and overcome.

51

Over time, people may have faith in you and they may lose it.
NEVER lose faith in yourself.

A long road becomes shorter
with every step.

Never stop learning.
Never stop loving.
Never stop living.

Realize that you don't
know everything,
trust those you ask to help you develop,
and learn more about who you are
and what you value most.

Hope is a beautiful thing.

Effort is understood and admired by many.

Hope + effort =
Making the impossible possible.

Look back on it all with a smile.
Look forward to it all with excitement.
Plant yourself here in the now.